GOLD MEDAL GUIDE

Golden tips for keeping your first

GUINEA PIG

AMANDA O'NEILL

Interpet Publishing

Editor: Philip de Ste. Croix
Designer: Phil Clucas MSIAD
Studio photography:
Neil Sutherland
Production management:
Consortium, Poslingford, Suffolk
Print production:
SNP Leefung Printers Ltd.
Printed and bound in the Far East

Published by Interpet Publishing,
Vincent Lane, Dorking,
Surrey RH4 3YX,
England

ISBN 978-1-84286-105-9

The Author   Amanda O'Neill was born in Sussex in 1951 and educated at the University of Exeter, where she read medieval literature. She has never lived without a variety of pets, ranging from rabbits and gerbils to giant snails and hissing cockroaches. Currently she lives in the Midlands with her husband and son, along with five dogs, a cat, Roborowski hamsters and a collection of coldwater fish.

The recommendations in this book are given without any guarantees on the part of the author and publisher. If in doubt, seek the advice of a vet or pet-care specialist.

Contents

INTRODUCTION

Guinea pigs are ideal first pets

Suitable for both children and adults, they are docile creatures which don't bite or scratch and respond well to gentle handling. They are cheap and easy to house and care for, and don't need specialist equipment such as lighting or heating. They are awake during the day, unlike many rodents. Given enough space and attention, they provide great entertainment with their gambols and companionable whistling calls. Poorly housed, neglected guinea pigs are not only unhappy but make boring pets, so before you adopt a guinea pig, be sure that you are prepared for the commitment.

Below: Big enough to be cuddly, small enough to handle easily, guinea pigs are also responsive and rewarding pets.

Pigs and Guinea have nothing to do with it!

They aren't pigs, and don't come from Guinea. They are rodents from South America, where they were domesticated at least 15 centuries ago as food animals. Their wild ancestors have died out, but in the Andes domesticated guinea pigs are still served for dinner. First imported into Europe in the 16th century, they soon became popular pets. Nobody knows why we call them guinea pigs. Possibly they were imported via Guinea, and nicknamed from their piggy squeals (or flavour). Purists prefer to call them cavies, from their scientific Latin name of *Cavia*.

Guinea pigs are not toys

Guinea pigs are only fun if you are prepared to put some time and effort into keeping them. Prospective owners need to be willing to spend some time each day feeding, watering, cleaning and handling their pet. You will need patience to tame a new guinea pig before you can enjoy each other's company. You will also need to be aware that they are living creatures with all the instincts of their wild ancestors. The human world is a strange environment, and only you can teach them to be comfortable within it.

GOLD MEDAL TIPS

LONG LIFESPAN
Guinea pigs are quite long-lived, averaging six to eight years – a few have even been recorded living to 12 years. So before you buy a guinea pig, be aware that this is a long-term responsibility.

SHOPPING LIST
Before you bring your new pet home, you will need (photograph left): a hutch, food bowl, water bottle, food, bedding and some form of exercise run. The guinea pig should be the last item on your shopping list.

GUINEA PIGS AND CHILDREN
Because they are so gentle, guinea pigs make great pets for children – but young children may not make great owners. If they are not old enough to understand that their pet doesn't enjoy being teased or chased, or that it will be injured if dropped, constant parental supervision is essential.

VARIETIES

Spots, stripes or checkerboard

The choice of colours is vast. 'Self' (plain-coloured) pigs include black, white, golden, red, lilac, beige and chocolate. Patterned pigs include pointed Himalayans (like Siamese cats), spotted Dalmatians, striped Harlequins and Magpies, checkerboard-patterned Tortoiseshells, and two-toned Dutch, whose coloured rump and eye patches contrast with a white middle and white facial blaze. There are also ticked or flecked breeds, including various shades of Agoutis and Roans.

Above: Cross-bred guinea pigs rarely grow such long coats as pedigree longhairs, but they still need some extra grooming.

Left: Most pet guinea pigs are of mixed ancestry, which provides endless (and often very handsome) variation of colour and markings.

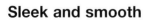

Sleek and smooth

The basic coat type is the smooth-coated guinea pig, with sleek short hair and these are bred in all colours. The Crested varieties have a whorl of hair on the forehead forming a little crest. In English Crested, the crest is the same colour as the pig's body; in American Crested, it is white and forms a contrasting 'star'.

Crowning glory

Long-coats come in all colours and several hair-styles. Peruvians are hairiest – their straight, floor-length mop makes it hard to tell which end is which. If you prefer to see the face, Shelties (Silkies) and their crested equivalents, Coronets, have shorter hair on the head, while Texels, Merinos and Alpacas have a permanent wave. All long-coated breeds need daily grooming to keep them clean, healthy and comfortable.

Other coat types

Variations on the short-haired theme include Satins, whose fur has a striking satiny sheen, and Rexes and Teddies, which have fuzzy, crinkly, outstanding coats giving a hedgehog-like appearance. Then there are Abyssinians, with rough, wiry hair about an inch long, arranged in a pattern of whorls ('rosettes'). There are even hairless pigs – Skinnies have a little hair on head and feet, and Baldwins are totally naked.

Below: The flecked coloration of the Agouti harks back to its wild ancestors.

CHOOSING

Where should I buy my guinea pig?

Most petshops stock guinea pigs, along with cages and other necessary equipment. Only buy from shops with well-housed, well-tended animals and knowledgeable staff. If the animals are over-crowded, dirty or nervous, go elsewhere. Alternatively, local breeders often advertise stock for sale, and the same rules apply. Animal shelters can also be a source of healthy but homeless guinea pigs seeking adoption.

How do I pick a healthy guinea pig?

Look for an alert animal with bright, clear eyes, a firm round body and healthy fur.

Avoid any pig which has runny eyes or nose, wheezy breath or a dirty bottom – or whose cage-mates display these signs. Guinea pigs are prone to parasitic infestations, so check the skin for dandruff, scabs and sores. Your new pet should be at least six weeks old, and males and females should be housed separately to avoid the risk of buying a pregnant female.

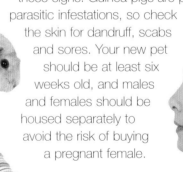

Right: Pick a pet which you can handle; wild, panicky youngsters will take a lot of taming.

A GUINEA PIG

One guinea pig – or more?

Guinea pigs are social animals and are unhappy in solitary confinement. Two or three will be happier together. In the wild, they live in family groups of females and young with one breeding male, and you can keep them in similar colonies (or as a mated pair) if you wish to breed them. However, this means a regular supply of babies needing new homes. For happy pets, think in terms of a pair of the same sex. Ideally you should look for two youngsters from the same litter to keep each other company.

Round but not fat

Sleek coat and healthy skin

Undamaged ear

Clear eye

Clean bottom

Clean nose

Sound paws

Regular breathing – not wheezing

Undamaged claws

Male or female?

Males or females make equally good pets. The safest combination is a pair or trio of females, or a neutered male with one or more females. Two males may live happily together if they are litter-mates who have never been separated, but unrelated males are likely to fight. Young guinea pigs are not always easy to sex, as they look very similar. Pressing gently on the lower belly above the genital organ will usually cause the penis to extrude if the animal is a male – ask for assistance if you are in any doubt.

HOUSING YOUR GUINEA PIG

The bigger the hutch, the better

Cramped cages mean dull lives for the inhabitants, and dull pets for their keeper. Many commercially produced hutches are too small and amount to prison cells rather than homes. To ensure that your pets have room to move, allow 65sq cm (7sq ft) for one guinea pig, adding about 20sq cm (2sq ft) for each additional animal. The hutch should have a smooth floor (not a wire base), and should have one end partitioned off to provide secluded sleeping quarters. Never place a hutch directly on the ground, but raise it on legs so that air circulates beneath, protecting both hutch and guinea pig from damp. Outdoor hutches need weather-proofing, using non-toxic wood preservatives, and a sloping roof to let rain drain off.

Above: The traditional outdoor hutch makes a cosy home, but may be cramped for space.

A home indoors

Indoor cages are usually made of plastic for ease of cleaning, with a deep tray base to prevent spillage of bedding. They may be sold as complete kits with food bowl, water bottle and hay rack, or you may need to buy these separately. Pick the largest cage you can accommodate, as some are too small to be kind. Plastic cages rarely offer the occupant any privacy, so add a hideaway nestbox to make your pet more comfortable.

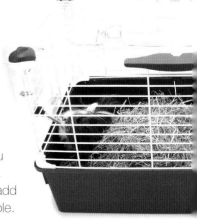

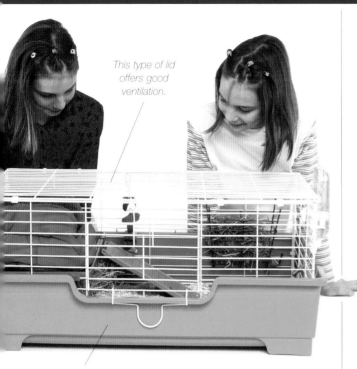

This type of lid offers good ventilation.

A deep base prevents spillage.

House pets

f you choose to locate your pet's cage
ndoors, choose the site carefully. The
noisiest, busiest room in the house
may be too stressful, while an out-of-the-way corner may
lead to neglect. It is important to avoid
draughts, direct sunlight and dramatic
changes in temperature.

A comfortable living-room
temperature for humans suits
guinea pigs just as well. Placing
the cage on a sturdy table or
stand makes access easier,
avoids draughts, and means that
you won't loom threateningly over
your pet when you approach.

*Left: An indoor cage – a more stimulating,
but potentially more stressful, environment.*

TANKS – NO THANKS!
Plastic tanks and aquariums
are not recommended for guinea
pigs. They have poor ventilation,
easily become over-heated,
and are difficult to clean. They
also isolate your guinea pig from
its surroundings, restricting its
environment by reducing
stimulation from smell,
sound and vision.

FLAWED FLOORS
Never house a guinea
pig in a cage with a wire floor,
such as are sometimes used for
rabbits or chinchillas. Guinea
pigs have sensitive feet and
cannot walk comfortably on wire
mesh. As well as developing
sore soles, they can also easily
trap their toes, causing foot
injuries and even broken limbs.

*Above: Tender soles and fragile
toes need a dry, well-padded
floor to walk on.*

GARAGE HAZARDS
A garage is not a suitable site
for your pet's cage. It is too hot
in summer, too cold in winter,
isolated from family activity,
and often damp and draughty.
There is also a very real risk of
toxic fumes from the family
car, which can be fatal.

THE ESSENTIAL

Bottles are best

A water bottle clipped to the front of the cage is better than a water bowl. It avoids risks of spillage or fouling of the water, and enables you to see at a glance whether your pet is drinking or not. Remember to change the water daily, and take the opportunity to check that the ball valve is working. Hold the bottle nozzle downwards and squeeze it gently. If no water comes out, the valve may be clogged or otherwise damaged. Some guinea pigs tend to chew the metal nozzle, and can crush it so that no water gets through.

Right: Clip on the water bottle so that the spout is at a comfortable height for use.

The perfect food bowl

Food bowls should be reasonably heavy and wider at the base than the top, so that they do not tip over easily. Metal bowls are often too lightweight, while plastic is not only light but dangerous, as your pet may chew it and cut itself on the sharp edges. Pottery bowls have the advantage of being heavy and easy to clean. Don't use too large a dish, or your guinea pig will sit in it and foul the food. Alternatively, you can choose a bowl with hooks which clip on to the cage front.

Right: A sturdy ceramic food-bowl is ideal.

EQUIPMENT

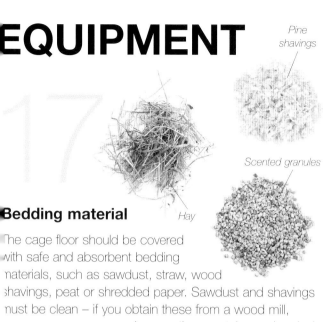

Pine shavings

Scented granules

Hay

Bedding material

The cage floor should be covered with safe and absorbent bedding materials, such as sawdust, straw, wood shavings, peat or shredded paper. Sawdust and shavings must be clean – if you obtain these from a wood mill, make sure they contain no chemical preservatives. Layers of news-paper spread over the cage floor before strewing the bedding on top provide extra absorbency. It's simple to roll up the paper with the used bedding inside. Inside the sleeping quarters, add plenty of hay for a soft bed and bedtime nibbles.

Left: Suitable bedroom nestboxes can be home-made from wood or even cardboard boxes, or you can buy more elaborate structures like this cosy woven ball, ideal for one guinea pig to snuggle down in.

CAGE FURNITURE
An empty cage offers little in the way of mental or physical stimulus. A cheap and effective solution is to place a few rocks, bricks or drainpipes (10cm/4in diameter) in the cage. These provide hiding places, climbing frames and rough surfaces to keep claws in good trim.

Clips onto cage bars

RACK NOT RUIN
A hay rack which clips on to the wall of the cage is useful to prevent hay (other than that in the sleeping quarters) from being trampled and soiled. It allows the guinea pig to pull down what it wants to eat at the time, keeping the rest safe for later.

DON'T LITTER!
Don't be tempted to use cat litter in your guinea pig's cage. It is tough on tender feet, and carries the further hazards of dust and added fragrance or deodorizer, which can damage your pet's respiratory system. There is also the risk that guinea pigs may nibble the litter and choke on the particles.

Carrot

Broccoli

Cabbage

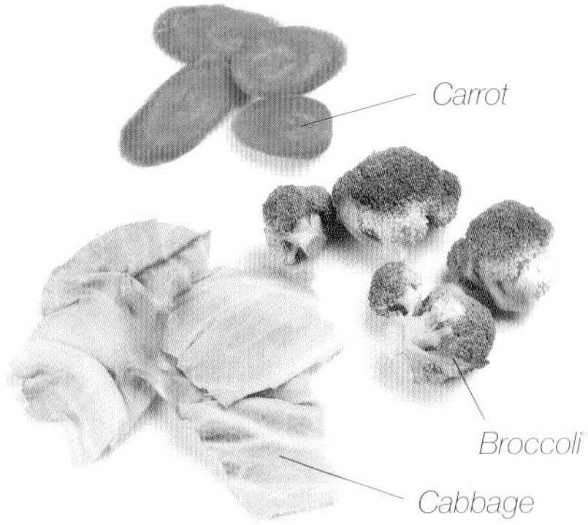

Vegetables and the vital vitamin

Unlike most animals (but like humans), guinea pigs cannot manufacture their own vitamin C but need to receive it from their diet. Pelleted food made specifically for this species (not rabbit pellets) contains added vitamin C, but your pet will also need daily portions of fresh foods such as cabbage, broccoli, carrots, grass, apples, dandelion greens, etc. Dark, leafy greens such as kale are particularly high in vitamin C.

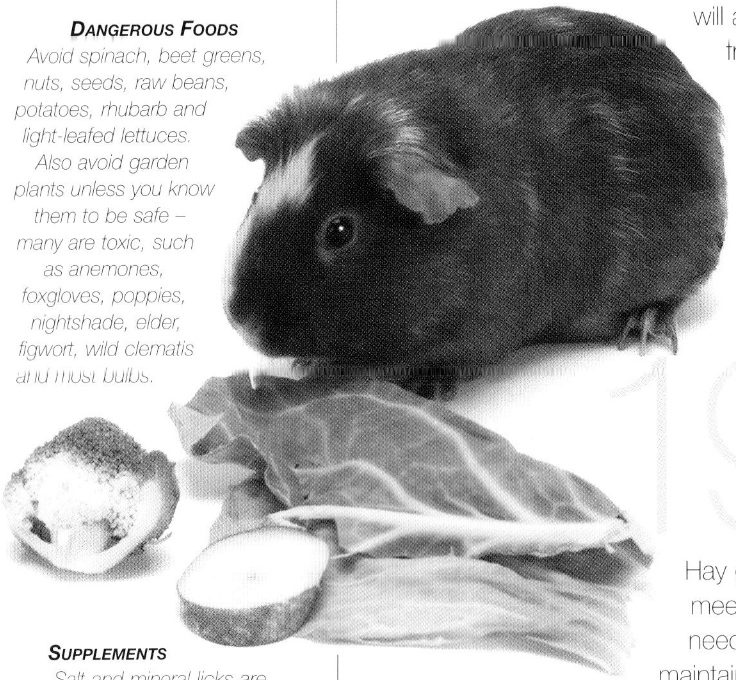

Hay should always be available

Hay goes a long way towards meeting your pet's nutritional needs, and its tough fibres maintain healthy gut movement and sound teeth. Nibbling hay also helps to reduce boredom and consequent behavioural problems. Good quality hay is essential. Avoid any that is dusty or musty-smelling, and always store hay where air can circulate – not in sealed plastic bags. Try different kinds – meadow hay, seed hay, kiln-dried grass – and see what your pet prefers. If in doubt, meadow hay is always a safe choice.

FOOD AND FEEDING

Pellets and cereals

As well as hay and greens, your pet needs dry foods. Guinea pig pellets are designed to fulfil their needs; mixes containing nuts, seeds and fruits may be too fattening. Cereals like oats and barley, or small pieces of toasted wholewheat bread, can also supplement the diet. However, guinea pigs are greedy creatures and will happily gobble themselves into obesity, so don't overfeed – about 60gm (2oz) dry food per day will suffice an active adult.

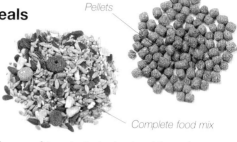
Pellets

Complete food mix

Right: Carrots combine healthy food with good exercise for the teeth.

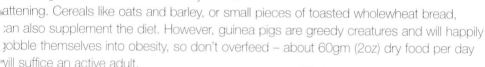

Water supplies

Fresh water must be supplied daily. Guinea pigs need, on average, 60-125ml (2-4fl oz) of water a day, though some will drink more and others less, especially if they obtain plenty of fluid from fresh foods. Water bottles should be kept out of direct sunlight to prevent algae growth, and washed regularly to keep them clean. In winter, water may expand when it freezes, so only half-fill the bottle so that it does not crack, and allow extra time to allow you to thaw out the ice and replace with fresh water.

Right: Change the water in your pet's bottle daily to prevent a build-up of dangerous bacteria.

15

TREATS AND TITBITS

Healthy snacks are best

Hand-feeding special titbits is a great way to increase your pet's confidence in you. Pet stores stock a wide range of chew sticks, nibbles and yogurt drops, which your pet may enjoy. Be careful when buying these, as some contain unshelled sunflower seeds which could choke your pet, while others are heavy on honey and therefore fattening. In any case, too many titbits are as bad for guinea pigs as for any other species. Your pet will be just as happy with healthy snacks, like apple slices or dandelion leaves.

Hang treats where they are easily reached.

Left: Food treats left on the cage floor soon become fouled; wedge them in the cage bars instead or hang from a suitable holder.

Apple

Pear

Banana

Grapes

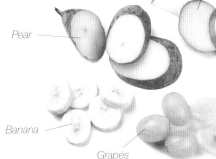

16

Guinea pigs need something to chew

Their teeth grow constantly throughout their lives, and a pig with nothing to chew will soon suffer from overgrown teeth which prevent him from eating. Vegetarian dog biscuits and dry toast make good tooth-grinders, but an even better answer to the guinea pig's dental demands is a length of branch wedged in his cage. Not all trees are suitable, but you cannot go wrong with wood from any fruit tree (apple, pear, plum, etc.). Leaves can be left on for an extra treat, but remove any fruit, especially if it is unripe.

NO SWEETS PLEASE
Chocolate and sweets designed for humans won't do a guinea pig any good at all. Sugary foods carry a high health risk: excess sugar is converted into fat, and a fat pig is not a healthy pig. Other snacks to be avoided include raisins, popcorn, nuts and cheese.

FIT NOT FAT
Overweight guinea pigs should never be placed on a drastic diet. Reducing the daily ration of pellets and cutting out fruit may help, but unlimited hay and vegetables must remain on the menu. Exercise is more likely to restore health, so make sure your pet has room to run and plenty to do.

Above: Hand-feeding helps to build up trust and friendship.

Fresh fruit should be given in moderation

Too much fruit will cause diarrhoea, which can be fatal – and fruit is also high in natural sugars, which won't do your pet's figure any good. However, a small daily portion (about a dessertspoonful) is beneficial. Apple, pineapple, banana, melon, pear, peach, grape and strawberry are all suitable, while half an orange with most of the pulp scooped out makes an appetising and healthy treat. Remove any seeds or stones before serving, and wash fruit to remove any traces of chemicals or preservatives.

TEACHING AIDS
Titbits can be very useful in training your pet. Although guinea pigs will not learn to perform tricks like some animals, you will want to teach your pet to look forward to seeing you and to enjoy being handled. Hand-feeding a tasty morsel every time you visit your guinea pig is the best way to achieve this.

PLAY AND EXERCISE

Guinea pigs need daily exercise

It is a good idea to schedule a playtime session (at least 15 minutes) outside the cage each day. For indoor guinea pigs, prepare a safe area such as the kitchen where they can explore. You will need to supervise them, and remove obvious hazards like electric wires. Outdoor exercise is ideal, combining keep-fit with fresh air and self-service snacks on the lawn – but a secure run is essential to protect your pet from getting lost, eating dangerous plants or indeed being eaten by a passing predator.

Above: Exercise and lunch in the fresh air keep your pets healthy while a secure enclosure keeps them safe.

Sunstroke can kill – and so can a chill

Hidey-holes offer peace and security.

When leaving your pet in his run, make sure he has shelter from direct sunlight. Remember that an area which is shaded in the morning may be fully exposed to the sun by afternoon. On hot days, draping a cloth over the run is a sensible safety measure. Guinea pigs also need protection from rain. Their fur is easily soaked, and a wet pig is a chilled pig. If your guinea pig gets wet, gently towel-dry his fur as much as possible and then keep him indoors in a box full of hay until he has dried out.

Left: This wooden shelter with its appealing pop-holes doubles as playhouse and cosy bedroom.

27

Guinea pig games

Encourage your pet to exercise by making his exercise area into a playground. Guinea pig games are simple, and require only quite basic equipment – cardboard boxes, brown paper bags and plastic drainpipes make ideal hidey holes, tunnels and obstacle courses. Scrambling over rocks, bricks or cinder blocks stretches muscles and keeps claws worn down. Arrange all accessories in the middle of the playground to leave the outskirts free for maximum running space. An active guinea pig is a healthy guinea pig.

SUMMER FUN
In mild weather, guinea pigs will benefit from spending much of the day outdoors in their run, so long as appropriate shelter is provided. However, they should always be taken back to their hutch at night to protect them from chills and the attention of passing foxes and other predators.

Plastic drainpipe

NO WHEELS
Exercise wheels and run-around balls as supplied for hamsters are not suitable for guinea pigs, even though some petshops stock guinea pig-sized versions. Guinea pigs are not built for this kind of exercise, which is bad for their backs. Hide-and-seek and obstacle scrambles are safer games.

HIGH JINKS
Guinea pigs can be very sedate, but when in high spirits they have bouts of wild activity, chasing about and jumping up into the air ('popcorning'). Novice owners may mistake these sudden vertical leaps for seizures, but they are simply an expression of well-being, the sign of a happy, healthy pig.

EYES AND EARS

Check eyes and ears weekly. Warning signs such as cloudy or watering eyes, crusty patches on ears or a build-up of wax or debris inside the ears should never be ignored. But don't worry about bald patches behind the ears – these are natural, and may be quite conspicuous in some individuals.

BOTTOMS UP!

It only takes a moment to check your guinea pig's bottom daily. A dirty bottom attracts flies and results in 'fly strike', with the unfortunate victim becoming infested with maggots. Good cage hygiene reduces the risk, but play safe with a daily inspection – especially vital in the case of long-coats.

Smooth-coated guinea pigs can groom themselves

However, it pays to help them out with this task at least once a week, using a small brush (a medium toothbrush is ideal if you don't have a proprietary one) or a fine-toothed comb with very gentle strokes. This helps to remove dead hair and also enables you to keep an eye on skin health, looking out for parasites, wounds and any other problems. It is also a great way to develop your relationship with your pet, who will come to look forward to the attention.

Right: Brush gently, first against the lie of the coat and then with it, to smooth it back into shape.

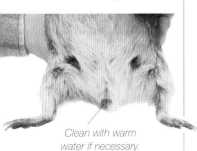

Clean with warm water if necessary.

BATHTIME

Guinea pigs don't need regular baths, but sometimes you need to clean up a dirty or smelly pet (usually a long-coat). Only use shampoo made specifically for small animals, and never put a damp animal back into a cold cage. Medicated shampoos may be also be prescribed for parasite infestations.

Long-coats need daily grooming

Their hair grows constantly (about 2.5cm/1in per month) and, without regular attention, quickly becomes soiled and matted. You will need a slicker brush and a wide-toothed comb, and a pair of fine-pointed scissors will be useful. Show specimens have their hair kept in paper wrappers to protect it; pets will be more comfortable if the hair is trimmed to a manageable length, especially around their bottoms and, if necessary, above the eyes.

GROOMING FOR HEALTH

Use a soft-bristled brush (right) for general purposes, or a slicker brush (left) for tangles.

Keep an eye on claws

Overgrown claws make walking difficult, and can eventually curve round to grow into the flesh. Make a claw check part of your weekly routine. If the claws need clipping, ask your vet to show you how. If you cut too short, you will cause pain and bleeding. With white claws, it is easy to see the pink 'quick' and cut below, but dark claws need extra care. If you do make a mistake, press the injured claw into a damp bar of soap to stop the bleeding.

Above: Claws should never be allowed to grow too long for your pet's comfort.

Guinea pigs' teeth grow throughout their lives

Normally, chewing keeps them down to the right length. But if a guinea pig lacks chewing opportunities, has a poor diet, or has inherited dental problems, teeth can grow too long, making eating tricky. A weekly dental check will help you to nip problems in the bud. Warning signs include eating difficulties, watering eyes and dribbling. Once a guinea pig's teeth have gone wrong, they will need regular attention from the vet.

Guinea pigs are always on the look-out

Their eyesight is adapted to spot predators, so they have eyes set wide apart and high on the head to give a good field of vision both sideways and upwards. They can't see detail or distant objects as well as we do, but they can see colour and are primed to catch the slightest motion – so you should avoid startling your guinea pig with any quick, sudden movements, especially with a new pet which does not yet know whether to trust you.

The sense of smell is important to guinea pigs

They have a much better sense of smell than humans, and it plays an important part in their social lives. Setting their own smell on their territory and on their cage-mates (which they do with urine and oily secretions from a scent gland at the base of the tail) makes them feel secure. The group smell of guinea pigs which live together is a social bond, while the smell of each individual tells the rest of the group his or her social position in the group.

Above: Guinea pigs depend on smell to locate and identify their food. Individuals vary in their sense of smell – most pick up the scent of dinner at some distance, others only when it is under their noses.

GUINEA PIG

Their hearing is nearly twice as good as ours

It is important to respect your pet's sensitive ears and recognize that loud noises (and high frequency sounds inaudible to us) can hurt their ears and cause them real distress. Don't expose them to loud music or noisy television shows. Keen hearing also means that they quickly learn to recognize sounds that indicate dinner time or treat time. They can distinguish their owner's footsteps from those of a stranger, and will squeal a greeting.

Guinea pigs are highly talkative

They communicate with each other, and with us, using a wide range of sounds as well as body language. Guinea pig owners soon become familiar with the loud chorus of squeals that greets dinner time, but guinea pigs also chatter, grunt, chirrup and gurgle. It is easy to distinguish between contented murmurs, frightened squeaks or angry teeth-chattering, and also to recognize postures, whether at ease, tense and watchful, or scared literally rigid.

HAPPY HABITS
Guinea pigs are creatures of habit and dislike change. They appreciate routine, with set mealtimes and exercise periods. Adults are often reluctant to try new foods, so it is a good idea to introduce youngsters to a range of foods while they are still open-minded enough to accept them.

INTELLIGENCE QUOTIENT
How bright are guinea pigs? The answer is that they are as bright as they need to be. They aren't good problem-solvers, and don't take naturally to training, but they quickly learn to associate patterns of events, for example linking the sound of the back door opening with the arrival of food.

SOCIAL STATUS
Status is important in guinea pig society. Males go for outright dominance, the winner driving other males away from his group. Females battle to establish rank. Once this is settled, high-ranking females take first pick of food or sleeping places and rarely bully their social inferiors.

Left: Youngsters use penetrating squeaks to call their mothers.

Don't hurry to handle a new pet

Guinea pigs are naturally very timid, so when you bring your new pet home, allow him a few days to settle in. He won't relax until his cage is familiar and full of his own scent. Once he feels at home, let him get used to your voice, and then to the smell of your fingers. A hand swooping suddenly overhead will look to him like a threat, so keep all movements slow and gentle. Let him learn to trust you before you try picking him up.

Left: Once your pet trusts your hands to offer titbits and strokes, he is ready to let you pick him up.

Reassure your pet by stroking its back

Getting down to it

It pays to get down to ground level when making friends with small animals. Towering over your pet from a great height makes you look threatening. When a new pet is out of his cage for an exercise period, sit or lie on the floor nearby with a tempting bit of greens near you. Later hold the titbit in your hand and wait for him to approach. Once a guinea pig associates your hand with treats, he is ready to accept, and even welcome, petting

HANDLING YOUR GUINEA PIG

How to pick up a guinea pig

Always use both hands. Slowly place one hand under your pet's chest just behind the forelegs (or around the chest from above if your hands are large enough), then gently cup his hindquarters in the other hand. Holding him firmly but without squeezing, raise him up to your chest or lap and hold him against your body so that he feels secure. Struggling pigs can be wrapped in a towel as a gentle restraint and for added security.

Support his weight at both ends.

Above: Guinea pigs hate to be dangled, so lift your pet quickly until he rests in a secure position.

Nips and nibbles

One of the many charms of guinea pigs is that they rarely bite. Some individuals will nibble because they like the salty taste of your skin. A few may use a gentle nip (usually without breaking the skin) to tell you that you are holding them uncomfortably or perhaps for too long. A guinea pig which bites is a stressed guinea pig, and punishing this behaviour will only serve to frighten him. Biters need patience and reassurance – and titbits come in handy too.

HEALTHCARE AND

Handling your pet daily is the best health check

You can spot symptoms such as itching and scratching, wheezy breath, lameness or telltale behavioural changes. Often by the time symptoms are evident a guinea pig may have been ill for a while. If he has stopped eating or drinking, or seems lethargic and huddles in a corner, he usually needs veterinary treatment as a matter of urgency. Failure to eat for as little as one day is extremely serious, as it can lead to liver damage.

Above: A fur coat may conceal lumps, bumps or sores which require attention, so make regular gentle check-ups.

Guinea pigs are prone to skin problems

44

Scratching, hair loss, dandruff or sores should always be taken seriously. These may be caused by parasitic or fungal infection, which cause considerable distress. Neglected skin problems can kill, as the affected animal may be too uncomfortable to eat or can suffer dehydration from weeping sores. Always take skin problems to the vet for diagnosis and prompt treatment. Medicated shampoos will often save the day.

Part the fur to inspect the skin.

Left: Regular skin checks enable you to notice warning signals, such as dandruff, hair loss or sore patches, before any funga or parasitic infestation becomes severe.

AILMENTS

Respiratory problems

Guinea pigs can catch colds from humans; they can also develop respiratory problems as a result of draughts, damp or poor hygiene. An odd sneeze is nothing to worry about, but continued sneezing, a runny nose or laboured breathing should be taken seriously. Separate snuffling guinea pigs from cage-mates to save the problem from spreading. Untreated colds often prove fatal, so seek veterinary help (usually in the form of safe antibiotics).

Below: Healthy guinea pigs love their food, so take any loss of appetite seriously.

Fresh food may tempt his appetite.

Tummy troubles

The commonest problem, diarrhoea, is usually caused by diet (stale or mouldy food, sudden diet change, or simply 'pigging out') and usually clears up after a few days on a dry diet. More serious cases (foul-smelling, black diarrhoea and a sore bottom) need the vet's attention. Also see the vet if your pet is constipated, with a hard, tight abdomen and general depression. This is likely to mean intestinal blockage (bloat) and again needs veterinary treatment.

45

46

GOLD MEDAL TIPS

SCURVY
Vitamin C deficiency causes scurvy (as in humans), resulting in lethargy, lack of appetite, weight loss, swollen joints and difficulty in walking, diarrhoea, and bleeding gums. A programme of vitamin C supplementation should be prescribed by the vet – and more attention paid to diet in the future.

Above: Fresh air and sunshine are good for your pets, but ensure that shade is available.

HEATSTROKE
Guinea pigs are very vulnerable to heat. Heatstroke victims should be wrapped in a thick towel which has been soaked in cold water and wrung out. Prevention is better than cure, so don't leave your pet unprotected in full sun, or shut in a poorly ventilated cage on a hot day.

ANTIBIOTIC HAZARDS
Many common antibiotics, including penicillin, are toxic to guinea pigs, causing diarrhoea and leading to a rapid death. Even 'safe' antibiotics can be dangerous if administered in the wrong quantity. Because of the risks, antibiotics should only be administered when prescribed by a vet.

BREEDING

Left: Breeding females need plenty of food to help them raise their numerous offspring.

The youngsters suckle for two or three weeks.

47 Think before you breed!

Before you go ahead, the three rules are: know why you have chosen to breed this litter, make sure you breed only from healthy well-handled animals, and know what you will do with the babies. Please, don't breed from your guinea pig unless you have a good reason to do so. There are already far more guinea pigs being bred than there are good homes for them, so don't add to the numbers of unwanted pets.

48 Guinea pigs breed all too easily

The sexes must be separated at four or five weeks of age, as they can mate this early – not a good idea! Never breed from youngsters under five months old, or breed a first litter from a female aged over ten months, as her pelvic bones will have fused and she may well die giving birth. Females can breed again immediately after giving birth, so remove the male before a litter is born to allow his mate a rest between litters.

ADVICE

49

Newborn guinea pigs are miniature adults

After an unusually long gestation period for rodents (60-72 days), they are born with fur and open eyes, and can run around soon after birth. Although they need their mother's milk for about three weeks, they also start eating solid food at one or two days old – so don't forget to increase food rations from the start. They are sexually mature at five or six weeks, although they will continue to grow for several more months.

ENORMOUS MOTHERS

A heavily pregnant female looks almost circular and will have almost doubled her weight by the time the babies are due. If the litter is a large one, she will look very uncomfortable. Handle females in the later stages of pregnancy as little as possible.

PREGNANCY CARE

Pregnant sows need extra food. In particular, they need double rations of vitamin C, so provide extra fruit and vegetables. Avoid any causes of stress. Remove the male if he shows signs of worrying his mate; otherwise he can stay with the female until the babies are due,

50

Right: Babies are born with teeth and digestive systems capable of tackling adult food.

Looking after babies

Guinea pigs are good, if casual mothers. If more than one female has young at the same time, babies will suckle from either mother at random. It is important to handle babies from the second day onwards, several times a day. This will not upset the mother in the least, and will ensure that the babies grow up tame and trusting of humans. Males should be moved to a separate cage at four or five weeks; females can stay with their mother.

HOW MANY BABIES?

The average litter size is two to four, but anything between one and eight is possible. First-time mothers often have smaller litters, and may lose their babies through inexperience, perhaps failing to remove newborn young from the birth sac, but they will usually cope better next time.

Further Information

Recommended Books

Barnes, Julia, *101 Facts About Guinea Pigs* (Ringpress Books, 2001)

Bawoll, Karen, *A New Owner's Guide to Guinea Pigs* (TFH Publications, 2001)

Behrend, Katrin, *Guinea Pigs (A Complete Owner's Manual)* (Barron's Educational Series, 1998)

Elward, Margaret and Ruelokke, Mette, *Guinea Piglopaedia* (Ringpress Books, 2004)

Evans, Mark, *Guinea Pigs (ASPCA Pet Care Guides for Kids)* (Turtleback Books, 2001)

Gurney, Peter, *The Proper Care of Guinea Pigs* (TFH Publications, 2000)

Gurney, Peter, *What's My Guinea Pig?* (Kingdom Books, 1998)

Henwood, Chris, *Pet Owner's Guide to the Guinea Pig* (Ringpress Books, 1999)

Mahoney, Myra, *The Really Useful Guinea Pig Guide* (Kingdom Books, 1999)

Page, Gill, *Getting To Know Your Guinea Pig* (Interpet Publishing, 1997)

Sigler, Dale L., *A Grown-up's Guide to Guinea Pigs* (Writer's Showcase, 2000)

Clubs

National Cavy Club (UK), 79 Thornhill Gardens, Hartlepool, TS26 0JF

American Cavy Breeders Association, PO Box 7522, Eugene, Oregon, USA

Recommended Websites

http://beanmakers.com

http://web.onetel.com/~petergurney

http://guinealynx.info

http://www.aracnet.com/~seagull/Guineas

http://guineapigs.info/sites.htm

Acknowledgements

The author and publisher would like to offer sincere thanks to Jackie Wilson and Emma Gillies of Rolf C. Hagen (UK) Ltd and Jason Casto and Colin Maidment of Superpet who generously supplied equipment for photography in this book. Thanks also to models Bronwyn and Stephanie McGuire and to Louise and Jacqui at Holmbush Farm, Faygate who kindly provided guinea pigs for photography, and to Peter Dean at Interpet Ltd for his help with photographic props.

Picture Credits

The photographs reproduced were taken by Neil Sutherland specifically for this book and are the copyright of Interpet Publishing. The photograph (top left) on the front cover was kindly supplied by, and is the copyright of:
Jane Burton, Warren Photographic.